SIMPLE CONTRACT LAW

A brief introduction to English Contract Law

Professor Mark Watson-Gandy

Cheerfully Illustrated
by the Rather Splendid
Mr Gordon Collett

To Lydia and Franklin

Contents

Preface		7
Chapter 1	Why English contract law?	11
Chapter 2	What is a contract?	14
Chapter 3	Necessary formalities to create a contract	17
Chapter 4	Valid, void, voidable and unenforceable contracts	23
Chapter 5	Offers	24
Chapter 6	Acceptance	34
Chapter 7	Consideration	38
Chapter 8	Privity	42
Chapter 9	Capacity	44
Chapter 10	Intention to create legal relations	48
Chapter 11	Terms	50
Chapter 12	Exclusion Clauses	54
Chapter 13	Misrepresentation	60
Chapter 14	Mistake	65
Chapter 15	Illegality	71
Chapter 16	Duress	74
Chapter 17	Undue Influence	77
Chapter 18	Discharge	80
Chapter 19	Remedies	85
Chapter 20	Epilogue	93
Glossary	Some common contract terms and what they do	95

PREFACE

Ever since the notion of contract first emerged from tort in the development of Common Law [1], English Contract Law reached paramount importance, probably even surpassing that of the Law of Torts. English law governs many international contracts, even where none of the parties is established in the UK or in the Commonwealth. Daily, these contracts are interpreted and scrutinised by businessmen who have to pay due consideration to the law of contract even though they are not lawyers. Frequently, English Contract Law is examined by overseas lawyers interested in comparative law and by students wishing to acquire a double legal culture, combining the virtues of common law and civil law. As a successful barrister and an inspiring professor, Mark Watson-Gandy has been the untiring apostle of Common Law on the continent sharing his refined approach to case law at the Faculty of Law of Nancy (Université de Lorraine) where a double BA in Civil Law and Common Law has now been taught for ten years. It is noteworthy that William Barclay, born in Aberdeenshire, was one of the first professors of Civil Law to be appointed in our Faculty in the XVIth century by Charles III Duke of Lorraine [2]. This gives clear evidence of the continuous cooperation amongst the academic legal community.

---

1   R. de Glanville, Tractatus de legibus and consuetudinibus regni Angliae (1188)

2   William Barclay, Professor of Law at Pont-a-Mousson and Angers" by Andrew F Stewart in Stair Society Miscellany V, ed H L MacQueen, Edinburgh 2006

The publication of *Simple Contract Law* appears to be the inevitable outcome of the passion that Mark Watson-Gandy has shown for sharing knowledge with the next generation of young professionals. The illustrations by Mr. Gordon Collett offer a highly effective way to capture the momentum of landmark cases and binding precedents, through an acute sense of observation in the detail of the drawings. But it would be a misconception to group this joyful book in the category of juvenile legal literature. Indeed, relations between words and illustrations have been a constant feature of legal literature, for example in the XVth century when commentators on Justinian Law would use illustrations (e.g., Bartollo of Sassoferato, *Consilia, quaestiones et tractatus*, Venice, 1495). Figurative arbores (trees) would also be used in Canon Law to present schemata for consanguinity, affinity and succession. If law is based on language, it also has to face the very limits of language. These limits are obvious when the moment comes to explain law to absolute beginners who do not share our linguistic conventions. These limits also become apparent when the moment comes to express one's own legal system and concepts in a foreign language. For these reasons, the drawings by Mr. Gordon Collett offer a supplementary key to unlocking the mysteries of English case law.

After an eager reading of this remarkable book, what would be the conclusions of a French professor and *avocat*, whose experience of English law has been through his activities as a shipping lawyer? Firstly, this book took me on a sentimental journey through case law, where joy has fortunately replaced nostalgia: after all, the cases illustrated here provide solutions that are still in force today. Secondly, it seems that the French and English judicial approaches to the law of contract may well be reconcilable. The reader of this book will discover that the principles from English judgements can indeed be efficiently summarised. Reciprocally, a British reader of current French cases, *en français dans le texte*, would discover that the *Cour de Cassation* has been adopting a new drafting style, to make judgements more accessible to readers who are not specialists in *Civil Law*. Beyond words, illustrations are a highly effective way to create a sense of community.

Olivier Cachard
Professor of Law, , Université de Lorraine
Honorary Dean of the Faculty of Law of Nancy
Avocat à la Cour et Arbitre international

Chapter 1
Why English contract law?

Ever since Man first traded a mammoth skin for a new spear, we have been entering into contracts with each other.

As time has gone by, contracts have become more complicated. We have needed rules to determine when we have a valid contract. We have needed skilled lawyers to commit the terms of our contracts to writing and then explain to us what the terms of the contracts mean. We have needed courts to resolve our disputes.

These days most international contracts choose to be interpreted under English law. This is in part because the English courts have a reputation for swiftly progressing cases and their judges are traditionally drawn from the very best and most experienced of the English barristers. Many cases before the English courts are now brought by litigants from overseas.

But this is also because English contract law is simple, convenient and straightforward. The terms the parties are bound by are those the parties set out in the contract and they don't need to check some other code or statute to find out what their contract means. Rather, the parties are, by and large, free to agree whatever they want. As a result, an English law contract tends to spell out the parties' rights and obligations in greater detail.

English law contracts have the attraction of giving the parties a greater degree of certainty and clarity. The terms the parties are bound by are what the parties chose when they struck their bargain rather than what a judge later decides would have been, in his view, reasonable.

Unlike many countries, English law does not rely on a civil code. English Contract Law instead has evolved over many centuries. Whilst small parts of it comes from laws made by Parliament, most of it is Common Law.

Common Law is law derived from decisions of judges. Where a judge finds a good solution to a problem, future judges will follow that solution so future litigants do not have to argue the same point again; this is known as following precedent. This does not prevent later judges from improving on the solution or finding exceptions to the rule where new issues have arisen.

Chapter 2
What is a Contract?

A contract is 'a legally binding agreement'. A mere promise, without more, does not create a contract.

"*Heads of terms*" (a preliminary note of proposed terms before the contract is drafted) does not create a contract. Nor does any arrangement in which neither party considers themselves legally bound to honour their promises (but rather hopes the other does); such an arrangement is sometimes known as a "*Gentlemen's Agreement*" (although this is not in truth an agreement at all and is rarely entered into by gentlemen).

Much like a cake mix, to create a valid contract one needs certain ingredients.

These are:

- An *Offer*
- *Acceptance* of the offer
- *Consideration*
- *Privity*
- *Capacity*
- An *Intention to create legal relations*
- No *vitiating factors* present.

Potential vitiating factors are:

- *Mistake*
- *Misrepresentation*
- *Duress*
- *Undue influence*
- *Illegality.*

You cannot create a valid contract if any of these ingredients are missing.

In the chapters that follow, I will explain a little more about each of these.

CHAPTER 3
NECESSARY FORMALITIES TO CREATE A CONTRACT

There are, as a general rule, no special formalities needed to create a valid contract. Contracts can be created by word of mouth, by the way the parties conduct themselves or in writing. Such simple contracts are known as *parol contracts* or simple contracts.

A written simple contract might look something like this:

THIS AGREEMENT *is made on 1ˢᵗ April 1404*

BETWEEN
Hieronymus Parsnip of 1 The Gardens, Beswick ["Mr Parsnip"] and
Cedric Alloysius Carrot of 1 Acacia Drive, Glossop ["Mr Carrot"]

WHEREAS the parties are desirous of entering into an agreement for the sale of the old master painting, "the Moaning Lisa", and Mr Parsnip is rather fond of boiled cabbage[3].

NOW IT IS HEREBY AGREED
That Mr Parrot will sell, and Mr Carrot will buy Mr Parsnip's old master painting titled "The Moaning Lisa" for Mr Carrot's cabbage on the above date.

---

3   This part of the contract is known as "the recitals"; it is not part of the contract but provides background to any future reader about why the contract was entered into.

1. Completion shall take place on the Windy Moor at the stroke of midnight on 1ˢᵗ April 1404, or such other place as may be agreed in writing by Mr Parsnip and Mr Carrot.
2. At Completion, Mr Carrot shall deliver or cause to be delivered a cabbage to Mr Parsnip and Mr Parsnip shall deliver or cause to be delivered to Mr Carrot the old master titled "The Moaning Lisa".
3. This agreement and any disputes or claims arising out of or in connection with it or its subject matter or formation (including non-contractual disputes or claims) are governed by and construed in accordance with the law of England and Wales. The parties irrevocably agree that the courts of England and Wales have exclusive jurisdiction to settle any dispute or claim that arises out of or in connection with this agreement or its subject matter or formation (including non-contractual disputes or claims).

IN WITNESS WHEREOF the parties have set their hands this date first above mentioned.

Signed:

Hieronymus Parsnip

Hieronymus Parsnip

Signed

Cedric Alloysius Carrot

Cedric Alloysius Carrot

If you want a more formal document, instead of a simple contract, you may choose to draft your contract in the form of a *deed*. Deeds are also known as speciality contracts.

A *Deed* might look something like this:

THIS DEED *is made on 1ˢᵗ April 1404*

BETWEEN
Hieronymus Parsnip of 1 The Gardens, Beswick ["Mr Parsnip"]
and
Cedric Alloysius Carrot of 1 Acacia Drive, Glossop ["Mr Carrot"]

WHEREAS the parties are desirous of entering into an agreement for the sale of the old master painting known as "the Moaning Lisa" and Mr Parsnip is rather fond of boiled cabbage[4].

NOW THIS DEED WITNESSETH AS FOLLOWS:
1. *That Mr Parrot agrees to sell, and Mr Carrot agrees to buy Mr Parsnip's old master painting titled "The Moaning Lisa" for Mr Carrot's cabbage on the above date.*
2. *Completion shall take place on the Windy Moor at the stroke of midnight on 1ˢᵗ April 1404, or such other place as may be agreed in writing by Mr Parsnip and Mr Carrot.*
3. *At Completion, Mr Carrot shall deliver or cause to be delivered a cabbage to Mr Parsnip and Mr Parsnip shall deliver or cause to be delivered to Mr Carrot the old master titled "The Moaning Lisa".*
4. *This agreement and any disputes or claims arising out of or in connection with it or its subject matter or formation (including non-contractual disputes or claims) are governed by and construed in accordance with the law of England and Wales. The parties irrevocably agree that the courts of England and Wales have exclusive jurisdiction to settle any dispute or claim that arises out of or in connection with this agreement or its subject matter or formation (including non-contractual disputes or claims).*

---

4   *This part of the contract is known as "the recitals"; it is not part of the contract but provides background to any future reader about why the contract was entered into.*

IN WITNESS *of which the parties have executed this agreement as a deed and it has been delivered on the day and year which first appears*

Signed as a DEED by:

Hieronymus Parsnip

Hieronymus Parsnip
In the presence of: Bertie Blind
Witness name: Bertie Blind
Witness address: Brixton Prison
Occupation: Burglar

Signed as a DEED by

Cedric Alloysius Carrot

Cedric Alloysius Carrot
In the presence of: Bertie Blind
Witness name: Bertie Blind
Witness address: Brixton Prison

Occupation: Burglar

In the olden days, a *deed* would have needed to be sealed with the parties' red wax seals stuck upon it and delivered. Today, it suffices that the document describes itself as a *"deed"*.

Although an instrument of some antiquity, deeds are not without their advantages. Contracts by deed do not need *consideration*. If someone breaches a contract by deed, you have a limitation period of twelve years to sue over the breach (instead of the normal six years).

There are certain contracts that must be made by deed. These include conveyances of land, leases of property extending over a period of more than three year or if you need to circumvent an absence of consideration.

Certain contracts must be in writing (but not necessarily by deed). These include bills of exchange, cheques and promissory notes[5], consumer credit agreements such as hire-purchase agreements[6], contracts of marine insurance[7], contracts relating to the sale or other disposition of land[8]

Certain contracts must even if they are not in writing themselves must at least be evidenced in writing, such as contracts of guarantee[9].

---

5   Bills of Exchange Act 1982

6   *Consumer Credit Act 1972*

7   *Marine Assurance Act 1906*

8   *Law of Property (Miscellaneous Provisions) Act 1989*

9   *s.4 of the Statute of Frauds Act 1677*

Chapter 4
Valid, void, voidable and unenforceable contracts

Valid contracts are contracts which the law recognises as fully binding on the parties.

Void contracts, by contrast, are contracts which are of no legal effect. Put shortly, although the parties may have hoped to create a contract, they have failed to do so. This might happen where the contract has been entered into due to one of the special categories of mistake, or because of the doctrine of illegality or some other public policy reason, or simply because the contract lacks one of necessary ingredients needed to make a contract such as consideration.

Voidable contracts are contracts which may be set aside by one of the parties to it. If no steps are taken to avoid the agreement then a valid contract ensues. Contracts entered into through fraud, misrepresentation or duress are voidable. Thus, a party who has entered a contract through the misrepresentations of another may, upon discovering he had been tricked, may choose to end the contract or, if it suits him, continue the contract, nonetheless.

An Unenforceable contract, by contrast, is an agreement which, although legal, cannot be sued upon for some reason. An example of this might be after the expiry of a limitation period where the time for enforcing the contract has lapsed.

Chapter 5
Offers

An offer is a promise, which is capable of acceptance, to be bound on particular terms. It may be made to a particular person, to a group of people or to the world at large[10].

Carlill v Carbolic Smoke Ball Co **(1893)**

The Carbolic Smoke Ball Company published advertisements in a newspaper, the Pall Mall Gazette, in November 1891 claiming "£100 reward will be paid by the Carbolic Smoke Ball Company to any person who contracts the increasing epidemic influenza colds, or any disease caused by taking cold, after having used the ball three times daily for two weeks, according to the printed directions supplied with each ball". Mrs. Louisa Elizabeth Carlill saw the advertisement, bought one of the balls and used it three times daily for nearly two months until she contracted the flu on 17 January 1892. When she claimed her £100, the Carbolic Smoke Ball Company refused to pay. The Court of Appeal found that the company was bound by its advertisement, which was construed as an offer which the buyer, by using the smoke ball, accepted, thus creating a contract.

---

10   *Carlill v Carbolic Smoke Ball Co (1893)*

If the offer is restricted then only the people to whom it is addressed may accept it; but if the offer is made to the public at large, it can be accepted by everyone. An offer cannot be too vague[11].

Scammel v Ouston [1941]

HC & JG Ouston ordered a van from G Scammel & Nephew Ltd with the price to be paid on 'hire-purchase terms' over two years. Unfortunately, Scammel used a number of different hire-purchase terms and the actual terms of Ouston's agreement were never actually fixed. The House of Lords ruled that there was no contract as the offer was too uncertain.

---

11 *Scammel & Nephew v Ouston [1941]*

Nor is a statement of a person's present intentions an offer[12].

Re Fickus (1900)

Mr Fickus told his prospective son-in-law that his daughter would inherit under his will. Discovering after his death that the father-in-law had left his estate elsewhere, the disappointed son-in-law sued. The Court held that the father-in-law's words were not an offer but simply a statement of his present intention which he could alter as he wished in the future.

Nor does the mere supply of information amount to an offer[13]

Harvey v Facey [1893]

Mr Facey had been carrying on negotiations with the Mayor and Council of Kingston, to sell Bumper Hall Pen in Jamaica to Kingston City. On 7 October 1893, Mr Facey was traveling on a train, when Mr Harvey, who wanted the property to be sold to him rather than to the City, sent Facey a telegram. It said, "Will you sell us Bumper Hall Pen? Telegraph lowest cash price-answer paid". Facey replied on the same day: "Lowest price for Bumper Hall Pen £900." Mr Harvey then replied in the following words. "We agree to buy Bumper Hall Pen for the sum of nine hundred pounds asked by you. Please send us your title deed in order that we may get early possession." Facey, however refused to sell at that price, at which Harvey sued. Harvey had his action dismissed at trial but won

---

12   *Re Fickus (1900)*
13   *Harvey v Facey [1893]*

his claim on the Court of Appeal, which reversed the trial court decision, declaring that a binding agreement had been proved. The Privy Council ruled that the indication of lowest acceptable price did not amount to an offer to sell. Rather, it is considered it to be an invitation to treat.

An invitation to treat is an invitation to others to make offers. The person extending the invitation is not bound to accept any offers made to them. Examples of invitations to treat include advertisements asking for tenders, goods in shop windows[14], share prospectuses inviting people to subscribe for shares in a company or goods on the shelves of supermarkets[15].

Fisher v Bell (1961)

Mr James Bell displayed a flick-knife in his shop window next to a price tag with the word "ejector knife 4 shillings". Chief Inspector George Fisher brought a prosecution against Mr Bell for "offering an offensive weapon for sale". The Divisional Court held Mr Bell had committed no offence because there was no "offer for sale" as goods displayed in a shop are merely an invitation to treat or invitation to trade.

---

14   *Fisher v Bell (1961)*
15   *Pharmaceutical Society of Great Britain v Boots Cash Chemists (1953)*

Pharmaceutical Society of Great Britain v Boots Cash Chemists (1953).

Boots Cash Chemists had just instituted a new system in their shops allowing customers to pick medicines off the shelves in the chemist and then pay for them at the till. Before then, all medicines were stored behind a counter and a shop employee would pick the potion requested from the shelf. The Pharmaceutical Society of Great Britain argued that this was an unlawful practice as a pharmacist needed to supervise at the point where "the sale is effected" and argued that the display of goods was an "offer" which was "accepted" when a shopper selected and put the medicine into their shopping basket. The Court of Appeal ruled that that the display of goods was not an offer. Rather, by placing the goods into the basket, it was the customer that made the offer to buy the goods. This offer could be either accepted or rejected by the pharmacist at the cash desk. Because the completion of the contract at the cash desk was in the presence of a supervising pharmacist, there was no violation of the law.

The express rejection of an offer ends the offer. A counteroffer is treated as amounting to a rejection of the offer[16].

Hyde v Wrench (1840)

Wrench offered to sell Hyde his farm in Luddenham for £1,000. Hyde offered £950, which Wrench rejected. Hyde then informed Wrench that he accepted the original offer of £1000. Wrench now refused to sell, and Hyde sued Wrench for breach of contract. The Court ruled that there was no contract: By making the counteroffer, Hyde rejected Wrench's offer. Once he had rejected Wrench's offer, he could not revive it later.

However, a request for information is not a counteroffer or a rejection[17].

---

16   *Hyde v Wrench (1840)*
17   *Stevenson v McLean (1880)*

Stevenson v McLean (1880)

Stevenson, Jaques & Co were iron merchants who purchased iron to sell on to third parties. Mr Maclean sent a telegram offering to sell to Stevenson Jaques & Co his iron warrants for "40 shillings, nett cash, open till Monday". On Monday morning, Stevenson Jaques at 9.42am asked what was the longest period that they would allow for payment. Hearing nothing, they accepted Maclean's offer at 1.34pm. Discovering later in a telegram that Maclean had sold the iron warrants to someone else, Stevenson sued him for breach of contract. The Court held there was a contract and Maclean was in breach; Stevenson's telegram at 9.42am was not a rejection of the offer but a mere inquiry about whether the terms could be modified. Maclean's attempt at revoking his offer was effective not when it was sent (1.25pm) but when it was received (after Stevenson Jaques & Co had accepted at 1.34pm) and thus did not prevent the contract coming into being.

An offer may expire at the end of a stated period if the offeror has set a time limit within which acceptance has to take place. An offer will lapse naturally after the passage of a reasonable time. An offer will lapse if the person to whom the offer was made dies or if the person making the offer dies provided the contract was one of a personal nature (such as the offeror offering to do something which requires his personal skill such as sing an aria or paint a picture). An offer may also be revoked by the offeror.

An offer may be revoked at any time before acceptance. Once revoked it is no longer open to the offeree to accept the original offer.

Routledge v Grant (1828)

Grant offered to buy Routledge's house and gave him six weeks to accept the offer. Within that period, however, Grant changed his mind and withdrew his offer. Routledge then accepted the offer, arguing that he had done so within the six-week period. The Court ruled that Grant was entitled to withdraw the offer at any time before acceptance.

To effectively revoke an offer, the person making the offer must make it known that his offer has been withdrawn. This is because the revocation of the offer is not effective until it is actually received by the offeree[18]: Communication of revocation may be made through a reliable third party[19].

Where the offer is an unilateral contract, revocation is not permissible once the offeree has started performing the task requested[20]; a unilateral contract is where one party promises something in return for some action on the part of another party (such as offering a reward).

---

18   *Byrne v Tienhoven (1880)*
19   *Dickinson v Dodds (1876)*
20   *Errington v Errington (1952)*

Errington v Errington (1952)

A father promised his son and daughter-in-law that he would convey a house to them when they had paid off the outstanding mortgage. After his death, the father's widow sought to revoke the promise. The Court ruled that the promise could not be withdrawn as long as the mortgage payments continued to be met.

Chapter 6

Acceptance

Once the person to whom the offer has been made accepts the terms offered, a contract comes into effect.

Both parties are bound.

Acceptance may be in the form of express words, either oral or written; or it may be implied from conduct. However, the acceptance must correspond with the terms of the offer.

Neale v Merritt (1830)

Merritt offered Neale to sell his property for £280. Neale replied saying that he accepted the offer, including £80 with his letter, and promising to pay the remainder by monthly instalments. The Court ruled that Neale had not concluded a contract with Merritt as his purported acceptance by adding a term that payment could be by instalments, did not correspond to the offer.

Thus, a counter offer does not amount to the acceptance of an offer[21].

Brogden v Metropolitan Railway Co (1877)

The Metropolitan Railway Co sent Mr Alexander Brogden, a coal merchant, a draft contract. Mr Brogden filled in some parts which had been left blank and inserted an

---

21   *Hyde v Wrench (1840)*

arbitrator who might decide any differences between them and then returned it, marked "approved". Metropolitan simply filed the documents and did nothing more. For a while, both acted according to the document's terms. But then some more serious disagreements arose, and Mr Brogden argued that no formal contract had been established. The House of Lords ruled that Mr Brogden's amendments amounted to a counteroffer, which had been accepted by Metropolitan when both parties acted on it.

However, silence, without more, cannot amount to acceptance.

Felthouse v Bindley (1863)

Mr Paul Felthouse, a builder, wrote to his nephew, Mr John Felthouse, after a discussion about buying the horse, "If I hear no more about it, I consider the horse mine at £30.15s." His nephew did not reply. He was busy at auctions on his farm in Tamworth. He told the man running the auctions, Mr William Bindley, not to sell the horse. But by accident, Mr Bindley did. Uncle Felthouse then sued Bindley in the tort of conversion on the basis that he now owned the horse. The Court of Common Pleas ruled that Uncle Felthouse did not own the horse as his nephew had not communicated his acceptance of the contract.

There are two important exceptions to this rule. The first is in the case of unilateral contracts where the person making the offer has waived the right to receive communication of acceptance and undertaking the envisaged performance is enough[22]. The second is where acceptance is envisaged as being through the postal service.

This latter exception is known as "the postal rule". The "postal rule" states that where parties have envisaged acceptance by post, acceptance takes place as soon as a properly addressed stamped letter is posted into the letter box (and is effective

---

22   *Carlill v Carbolic Smoke Ball Co (1893)*

even though the letter doesn't arrive!)[23]. The postal rule does not apply to instantaneous forms of communication, such as the telephone, telegrams, facsimile, or email; for each of these, the offeror must actually receive the acceptance for it to be effective[24]. Moreover, a person making an offer is free to insist, at the time he makes that offer, that the postal rule is not to apply and that acceptance will only be effective when it is received[25].

---

23   *Adams v Lindsell (1818)*
24   *Entores v Miles Far East Corp (1955)*
25   *Holwell Securities v Hughes (1974)*

CHAPTER 7

CONSIDERATION

An essential ingredient of any contract is that both sides must provide *consideration* to the other, *Consideration* means the price paid for a promise. It has been defined as 'some benefit to the promisor or detriment to the promisee' or the *quid pro quo*.

Consideration may be an asset, a service, or even forbearance, that is to say some non-action, or the relinquishing of some right (for example, agreeing not to bring a court case against the other. *Consideration* must be sufficient but need not be adequate. Lawyers seeking to express a nominal but perfectly legal valid consideration set the price as "a peppercorn payable if demanded".

Chappell & Co v Nestlé Co [1960]

Nestlé offered to sell records at a discount price to anyone who sent in three 6 penny chocolate bar wrappers. Chappell & Co held the copyright in one of the recordings, "Rockin Shoes". Chappell argued that the wrappers formed part of the price and they were entitled to royalties on this part of the price too. The House of Lords agreed and ruled that the wrappers could amount to valid consideration; this was even though the wrappers were worthless, and Nestlé threw them away when they received them.

Contracts by deed do not need *consideration* (the wax seal symbolically provided the parties' "price").

Consideration may be provided at the time of contracting or at some time in the future. Things that have already been given or historical action however do not amount to good consideration.

Past consideration is, thus, no consideration. There are some exceptions to the rule, namely bills of exchange[26], the principle that time barred debts become enforceable again if they are acknowledged in writing[27] and also where the claimant performed work at the request of the defendant with the expectation of his payment, then any subsequent promise to pay will be enforceable.

Discharge of a pre-existing public duty is not valid consideration however consideration may arise if the person does more than his public duty requires[28]. Similarly, the performance of a contractual duty cannot be reused to found consideration for a new contract[29].

Stilk v Myrick (1809)

When two members of the crew deserted when the ship docked at Cronstadt, the ship's captain promised Stilk and the other remaining members of the crew that they would share the deserters' wages if they completed the voyage to the Baltic and back. Stilk completed the voyage but Myrick, the owner of the ship, refused to honour

---

26   s. 27, Bills of Exchange Act 1882
27   s. 29 Limitation Act 1980
28   *Harris v Sheffield United FC (1987)*, *Glasbrook v Glamorgan County Council (1925)*
29   *Stilk v Myrick (1809)*

the promise made by his captain. The Court ruled that Stilk could not enforce the captain's promise as Stilk had provided no consideration as he had not done more than that which he was already obliged to do.

However, performance of a contract duty owed to one person can amount to valid consideration *for the promise made by another person*[30].

Shadwell v Shadwell (1860)

Mr Shadwell's uncle Charles promised him that if he married, he would pay his nephew £150 per year, until his earnings as a chancery barrister reached 600 guineas a year. In fact, Mr Shadwell was already engaged to Ellen Nicholl. On the death of Uncle Charles, Mr Shadwell

---

30   *Shadwell v Shadwell (1860)*

claimed his uncle had not paid in full, but his Uncle's estate refused to pay on the ground that Mr Shadwell had given no consideration for the promise to pay. The Court ruled that going through with the marriage was sufficient consideration for the uncle's promise, even though the nephew was already contractually bound to his fiancée.

Under Common Law, part payment cannot amount to satisfaction of a debt unless further consideration is given[31]. The rule may be circumvented by payment in kind, payment by agreement, before the due date of payment, payment at a different place, payment of a lesser sum by a third party or under a composition arrangement (where all creditors mutually agree to accept part-payment of their debts).

Pinnel's case (1602)

Pinnel sued Cole for a bond of £8, 10 shillings. Cole, however, argued that Pinnel had accepted £5, 2 shillings and 2 pennies in full satisfaction for the debt. The Court ruled that this was not enough to discharge the debt, although had payment been in kind (rather than in money) such as by "a hawk, horse or robe" that would have sufficed.

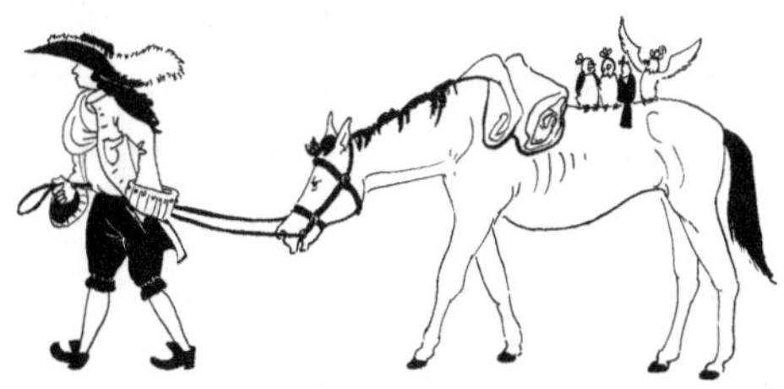

---

31   *The Rule in Pinnell's Case*

Chapter 8

Privity

Privity means that a contract can only impose rights or obligations on persons who are parties to it. Non-parties cannot enforce the contract.

Dunlop v Selfridge [1915]

Dunlop sold tyres to Dew & Co, who were wholesalers, on terms that they would not sell for less than the lowest price fixed by Dunlop, agreeing to bind any purchasers not to sell below that price. Dew & Co resold tyres to Selfridge on the same terms. Selfridge broke the pricing agreement and sold the tyres at a discount. Dunlop sued Selfridge however the Court ruled that Dunlop's claim failed for want of privity; Dunlop was not a party to the agreement between Dew & Co and Selfridge.

Where it is intended that a benefit be given to a third party, there are a number of ways around the rule of *privity* and to give the beneficiary enforceable contractual rights. For instance the beneficiary could sue in some other capacity (enforcing a party's rights as his agent or trustee), the benefit of the contract could be assigned under a collateral contract or by an express term of the contract[32].

---

32   *Contracts (Third Party Rights) Act 1999*

Shanklin Pier v Detel Products (1951)

Shanklin Pier entered into a contract with painters to paint their pier with Detel paint after Detel Products had assured them that their paint would last for at least seven years without deterioration. In fact, the paint peeled within three months. Shanklin Pier sued Detel Products for breach of contract. The Court ruled that although Shanklin Pier had no right of action under the contract with the painters (as there was no privity), a collateral contract had arisen between Detel and Shanklin Pier as Shanklin Pier had agreed to use Detel paints in the main contract on the basis of Detel's promise of their suitability.

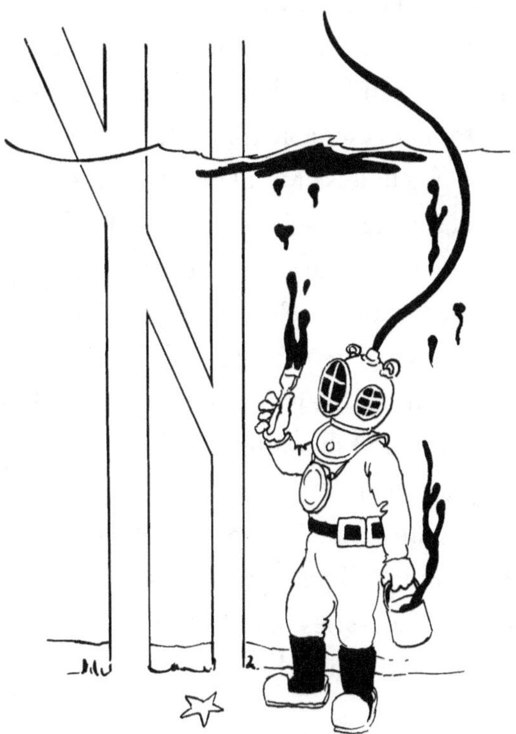

Chapter 9

Capacity

Capacity refers to a person's ability to enter into a contract. All adults of sound mind have full capacity to enter into a contract.

There are three exceptions to this rule: minors, patients and drunken people.

Minors

A minor is someone under the age of 18 years.

Depending on the nature of the contracts with a minor, the contract may be valid, binding until he repudiates whilst a minor or within a reasonable time after becoming 18 years of age or not binding unless or until he ratifies them once aged 18.

Valid (and thus binding) contracts with a minor are those for the supply of necessaries, contracts of apprenticeship (if they have an educational element), contracts for education, contracts of service (if beneficial to the minor) and for the sale of a minor's goods (if the goods are delivered). If necessaries are sold and delivered to a minor, the minor must pay a reasonable price for them[33].

Necessaries are defined as goods suitable to the condition of life of the minor and his actual requirements at the time of sale. A minor's necessaries have been held to include also the necessaries of his wife and children.

---

33   *Section 3 Sale of Goods Act 1979*

Necessaries have been held to include:
- legal services
- medical services
- the costs of a spouse's funeral
- wedding rings
- a bicycle
- car hire
- regimental uniform.

Things that have been held not to be necessaries include:
- 11 fancy waistcoats
- flying lessons for a law student
- large quantities of tobacco
- expensive dinners for a student friend
- a collection of snuff boxes
- a second-hand sports car.

Contracts that have been held to be binding unless repudiated are contracts under which the minor acquires an interest of a permanent nature, such as subscription to shares, leases or sales of land, partnership. However, whilst the minor holds such an interest, the minor is liable to pay any calls, rent or partnership debts that arise.

All other contracts are not binding on the minor until they have been ratified on or after his 18th birthday. This covers contracts like loans, sales of non-necessary goods and trading contracts. If the contract is unenforceable and the Court considers that it is just and equitable, the Court may require the minor to transfer back any property acquired by the minor or any property representing it under such a contract[34]

Patients

If at the time of contracting, the patient was so insane that he did not know what he was doing, and the other side knew him to be so insane[35] or ought to[36], the contract is voidable at the patient's option. The burden of proof on a person alleging incapacity is to show that he was incapable of understanding the nature of what he was doing and did not understand what the contract meant or said[37]. He still will be required to pay a reasonable price for necessaries[38]

---

34   *Section 3 Minors Contracts Act 1987*
35   *Imperial Loan v Stone (1892)*
36   *Dunhill v Burgin (2014)*
37   *Fehily v Atkinson [2016]*
38   *Section 7 Mental Capacity Act 2005*

Drunkenness

If at time of contracting, the party was so intoxicated that he did not know what he was doing, and the other side knew him to be so drunk[39] or ought to[40], the contract is voidable at his option. The contract thus can be ratified when sober. If necessaries are sold and delivered to a person who is incompetent by reason of drunkenness, he must still pay a reasonable price for them.

39   *Imperial Loan v Stone (1892)*
40   *Dunhill v Burgin (2014)*

CHAPTER 10
INTENTION TO CREATE LEGAL RELATIONS

The courts will only enforce those agreements which the parties intended to have legal effect.

The law presumes that the parties do not intend to give domestic or social relations legal effect. Thus, a court will assume arrangements between parents and children are not intended to be enforceable[41]. This may be rebutted.

Other examples where the presumption arises and which (absent evidence to the contrary) will not normally be enforceable in the courts, include collective agreements, such as agreements between employers and trade unions, and letters of comfort from parent companies assuring that they intend to continue to provide financial backing for subsidiaries[42].

"Sales puffs" in advertisements, boasts which could not be seriously believed to be meant, are similarly not assumed to be given legal force[43].

---

41   *Jones v Padavatton (1969)*

42   *Kleinwort Benson v Malaysian Mining Corp (1989)*

43   *Weeks v Tybald (1605)*

Weeks v Tybald (1605)

Mr Tybald advertised that he would give £100 to "him that should marry his daughter with his consent". The Court held this was mere puff as nobody could have reasonably expected that Mr Tybald was bound by his words, having merely intended to "excite" prospective suitors.

CHAPTER 11
TERMS

Terms in a contract can be classified as one of three types:

- A "condition" is a fundamental part of the agreement; it is something which goes to the root of the contract. Breach of a condition gives the innocent party the right either to terminate the contract and refuse to perform their part of it or go through with the agreement and sue for damages[44].

- A "warranty" is a subsidiary obligation which is not vital to the overall agreement; and does not totally destroy its efficacy[45]. Breach of a warranty does not give the right to terminate the agreement. The innocent party has to complete their part of the agreement and can only sue for damages.

- An "innominate term" covers the situation where if the innocent party is deprived of 'substantially the whole benefit of the contract', then the right to repudiate will be permitted even if the term might otherwise appear to be a mere warranty[46].

---

44   *Poussard v Spiers (1876)*
45   *Bettini v Gye (1876)*
46   *Hong Kong Fir Shipping Co v Kawasaki Kisen Kaisha [1962]*

Those Terms may be express or implied. Express terms are the terms which the parties themselves state are to be in the contract. Certain terms, which are not expressly stated, may be implied and are nonetheless treated as part of the contractual agreement.

Terms may be implied by (1) statute, for example that the goods being sold are of satisfactory quality and are fit for the purpose for which they are being sold[47] or that they would match their description[48] or that work contracted for will be undertaken with reasonable care and skill[49] and within a reasonable time[50] (2) by custom or trade use[51] (3) or by the courts.

The courts will look to trade usage or custom where the contract is silent on the issue and provided that it would be inconsistent with the express terms of the contract.

47   s 9 and 10, *Consumer Rights Act 2015*
48   s 11, *Consumer Rights Act 2015*
49   s 49, *Consumer Rights Act 2015*
50   s 52, *Consumer Rights Act 2015*
51   *Hutton v Warren (1836)*

Hutton v Warren (1836)

Mr Hutton, a farm tenant, who lived in Wroot in Lincolnshire, claimed that it was the custom of the country that the landlord would give a reasonable allowance for seeds and labour to keep the land arable, and that he would leave manure should the landlord wish to purchase it. The Court ruled that given the lease was silent on this point, it was entitled to look at evidence of local custom and usage when interpreting the lease and found that the farm tenant was entitled to a reasonable allowance for his seed and labour on quitting his tenancy in respect of unharvested crops on the land.

The courts will imply a term where it is obvious and necessary in order to give it business efficacy (but not where it would be merely desirable to do so); so that if at the time of contracting some "Officious Bystander" were to suggest some express provision for it in the contract, the parties would have testily supressed him with a common "Oh, of course".[52]

The Moorcock (1889)

The owners of the ship called *The Moorcock* contracted for space at a wharf owner's jetty in order to unload the ship's cargo. While docked, the tide went down to a point where the hull of the ship hit a ridge, causing damage to the ship. The owners argued that the wharf owners were responsible to ensure that his vessel would remain safe while docked. The wharf owners defended the claim, arguing that there were no provisions in the contract

---

52   *Shirlaw v Southern Foundries [1940]*

to ensure the vessel's safety. The Court of Appeal ruled that whilst no express term existed, a term that the jetty would be a safe place to dock could be implied to give the contract business efficacy.

CHAPTER 12
EXCLUSION CLAUSES

An exclusion clause is a term in a contract which tries to exempt, or limit, the liability of a party in breach of the agreement.

When considering whether an exclusion clause is effective, a court will ask itself: Has the exclusion clause been incorporated into the contract? Does the exclusion clause effectively cover the breach? Is it reasonable? Next, the court will consider the constraints applied by statute, first, by the Unfair Contract Terms Act 1977 and, more recently, by the Consumer Rights Act 2015.

A clause or term may be incorporated into a contract by a variety of means. It may be incorporated by signature, by notice, by reference to another document or incorporated through a previous course of dealings.

Plainly if a person signs a contract, he clearly demonstrates his acceptance of its terms. Indeed, if a person signs a contractual document, then they are bound by its terms, even if they did not read it[53].

L'Estrange v Graucob (1934)

Miss Harriet L'Estrange owned a café in Llandudno. She ordered a cigarette machine from two travelling salesmen from F Graucob Ltd. The machine persistently jammed.

---

53   *L'Estrange v Graucob (1934)*

She sued the manufacturers, Graucob, saying they were in breach of an implied term that the machine would be reasonably fit for its purpose. Graucob denied that the term could be implied, arguing that the contract which she had signed contained a clause in small print stating that "any express or implied condition or warranty, statutory or otherwise, not stated herein is hereby excluded." The Court of Appeal ruled that the fact Miss L'Estrange had signed it made the fact she had neither read nor was aware of the exclusion clause irrelevant. Absent fraud or misrepresentation, the signature binds the party and it is immaterial whether she had read the contract or not. The exclusion clause stopped the term from being implied and thus F Graucob Ltd was not in breach of contract despite delivering a faulty machine.

Contractual terms may also be introduced if they are displayed in a notice or a sign on display to the contracting parties. For incorporation of terms by notice, the exclusion clause must be introduced before or at the time of the contract.

Olley v Marlborough Court Hotel (1949)

Mrs Olley was a long staying guest at the Marlborough Court Hotel. Whilst Mrs Olley was out for the evening, a thief had entered the hotel. Seeing that the porter was distracted with dusting a plaster bust of the Duke of Marlborough, the thief snatched a key from the reception desk and, using it to gain access to Mrs Olley's room, stole her fur coat. Mrs Olley sued the hotel. The Hotel attempted to disclaim liability based on a notice displayed on the back of the lavatory door in Mrs Olley's room, which stated that "the proprietors will not hold themselves liable for items lost or stolen unless handed to the manageress for safe custody". The Court of Appeal ruled that the hotel could not rely on the exclusion clause to escape from liability as the contract was formed at the reception desk when Mrs Olley first checked in. As at that time she contracted, Mrs Olley had not yet been given the keys to her room, she could not have been aware of the clause, which is what would have been needed to incorporate it into the contract.

Not only must the term be introduced before or at the time of the contract, the court requires that the notice given of the exclusion clause must be reasonable so that the party bound by the exclusion clause is made sufficiently aware of the clause at the time of contracting.

Thornton v Shoe Lane Parking Ltd (1971)

Mr Francis Thornton, "a free-lance trumpeter of the highest quality", drove to the entrance of Shoe Lane multi-storey car park, before attending a performance at Farringdon Hall. He took a ticket from the machine and parked his car. On the ticket it said, "this ticket is issued subject to the conditions of issue as displayed on the premises". Indeed, on the car park pillars near the paying office there was a list of conditions, one excluding liability for "injury to the Customer… howsoever that loss, misdelivery, damage or injury shall be caused". On his return to the car, he was seriously injured by another car and sued for damages. Shoe Lane Parking relied on the exclusion clause. The Court of Appeal held that the more onerous the exclusion clause, the better notice of it needed to be given. Moreover, the contract was already concluded when the ticket came out of the machine, and so any condition on the ticket could not be incorporated in the contract.

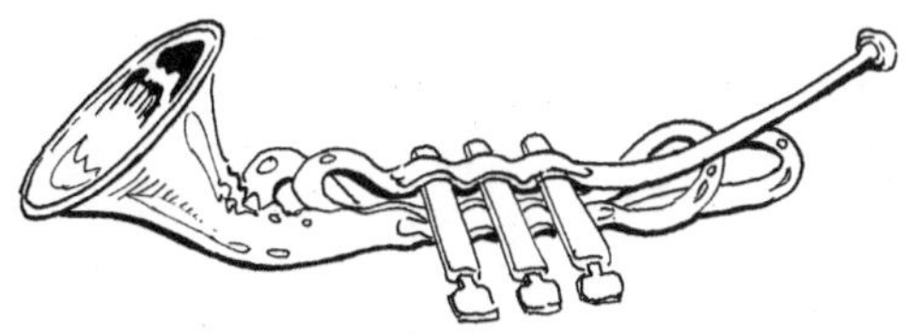

Where the parties have had previous dealings on the basis of an exclusion clause, that clause may be included in later contracts, but it has to be shown that the party affected had actual knowledge of the exclusion clause[54].

---

54   *Spurling v Bradshaw (1956)*

If the exclusion clause has been incorporated into the contract, then it is necessary to show that the exclusion clause covers the breach that has occurred. Under the *contra proferentum* rule, the court will construe any doubt as to the meaning of the words against the party relying on their exclusion clause to escape liability[55]. Thus, to exclude liability for their negligence, the person drafting the clause must say so expressly[56].

In consumer contracts, unfair terms and unfair notices are not binding on the consumer (unless the consumer chooses to rely on them); terms and notices are unfair if, contrary to the requirements of good faith, the exclusion clause causes a significant imbalance in the parties' rights and obligations to the detriment of the consumer[57]. The Consumer Rights Act 2015 concerns contracts between a trader and a consumer; a consumer is an individual acting wholly or mainly outside his trade, craft and profession[58]. A trader cannot exclude liability for death or personal injury caused by negligence[59].

---

55   *Houghton v Trafalgar Insurance (1953)*

56   *Hollier v Rambler Motors Ltd (1972)*

57   *Section 62 Consumer Rights Act 2015*

58   *Section 2(3) Consumer Rights Act 2015*

59   *Section 65 Consumer Rights Act 2015*

In relation to things done in the course of a business, where one person deals on another's standard written terms of business[60] or terms in relation to the sale or hire purchase of goods[61], a party may not exclude or restrict liability unless the party relying on the clause can show it satisfies the requirement of reasonableness[62]. A party cannot exclude liability for death or personal injury cause by negligence[63].

---

60   *Section 3 Unfair Contract Terms Act 1977*
61   *Sections 6 and 7 Unfair Contract Terms Act 1977*
62   *Section 11 and Schedule 2, Unfair Contract Terms Act 1977*
63   *S 2, Unfair Contract Terms Act 1977*

Chapter 13
Misrepresentation

If a party was induced into entering into a contract by a misrepresentation made by the other, he may rescind the contract.

A misrepresentation is a statement of material fact made to the other party before the contract was entered into which was false or misleading and which induced the other party to enter into the contract. A false statement of opinion is not a misrepresentation. Nor are sales puffs. Nor are statements as to future conduct or future intentions. Nor are statements about the law.

Silence will not normally amount to a misrepresentation, however exceptions to this occur where a half-truth has been told[64] or there has been a change of circumstances or where there is some other duty to disclose, such as because there is a fiduciary relationship or with contracts *uberrimae fidei* (of the utmost good faith) – such as insurance policies.

With v O'Flanagan [1936]
Dr O'Flanagan told Mr With truthfully in January 1934 that his medical practice had takings of £2000 per annum. However, by May 1934, the takings had fallen to £5 a week because Dr O'Flanagan had become ill. The contract was signed with Mr With to buy the medical practice,

---

64   *Nottingham Patent Brick & Tile Co v Butler (1886)*

but Dr O'Flanagan did not disclose the change in circumstances. The Court of Appeal ruled that Mr With could rescind either because there was a duty to point out the change in circumstance or because the representation continued till the point when the contract was signed; a 'representation made as a matter of inducement to enter a contract is to be treated as a continuing representation.'

A misrepresentation may be in writing, by words or by conduct.

Spice Girls v Aprilia World (2000)
Aprilia, who manufactured mopeds, agreed to sponsor the Spice Girls on their concert tour having seen all five members of the band at its promotional photo shoot. Ginger Spice was to leave the band later that month. The Court of Appeal ruled that the appearance of all five Spice Girls in the commercial amounted to a representation by conduct by all five band members that they would all participate in the tour which had induced Aprilia to enter the contract.

A misrepresentation may be innocent, negligent or fraudulent. Fraudulent misrepresentation occurs where the false representation is made knowingly or without believing it to be true or recklessly careless as to whether it is true or not[65]. Where a party has been induced to enter a contract by fraudulent misrepresentation, he may rescind the contract and claim damages.

Derry v Peak (1889)

Mr Derry was a director of the Plymouth, Devenport & District Tramway. The Tramway was allowed to run horse powered trams or, with the consent of the Board of Trade, using steam power. Believing consent to be a mere formality, the Tramway issued a prospectus claiming steam power would be used. However, the Board of Trade refused permission. Sir Henry Perry, representing the disgruntled new shareholders, sued claiming that the prospectus contained a fraudulent misrepresentation. The House of Lords ruled for there to be deceit or fraud it must be shown that a defendant (i) knows a statement is untrue, or (ii) has no belief in its truth, or (iii) is reckless as to whether it is true or false. The Court found that that there was no fraudulent misrepresentation because it could not be shown that Mr Derry believed the statement was false.

---

65   *Derry v Peak (1889)*

Negligent misrepresentation at Common Law occurs if the defendant carelessly makes a false statement to the claimant and it is reasonable to assume that the statement will be relied upon and there is a special relationship between the parties. A special relationship will arise if the person making the statement has special knowledge or skill in relation to the subject matter of the contract and can reasonably foresee that the other will rely upon it[66].

Hedley Byrne v Heller (1963)

Hedley Byrne, an advertising agency, asked Heller & Partners Ltd, a bank, for a reference in respect of one of their customers, Easipower Ltd. The Bank replied that Easipower Ltd could be "considered good for its ordinary business engagements" when in fact it could not. Easipower Ltd went into liquidation owing Hedley Byrne £17,000. The House of Lords ruled that the reference was a negligent misrepresentation by the Bank.

A claim for negligent misrepresentation may also be claimed under the Misrepresentation Act 1967. Where a person has entered into a contract induced by a misrepresentation and has been caused loss, the person making the misrepresentation will be liable unless he proves that he had reasonable grounds to believe and did believe up to the time the contract was made that the facts represented were true. Where a party has been induced to enter a contract by negligent misrepresentation, he may rescind the contract and claim reasonably foreseeable damages.

66   *Esso Petroleum v Mardon (1976)*

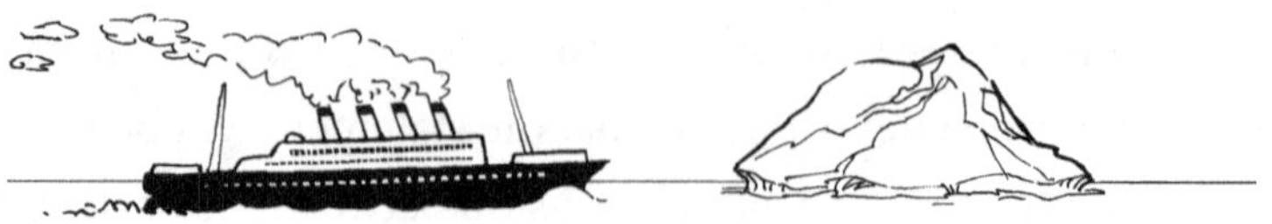

An innocent misrepresentation occurs where the party making it believes that it is true and has reasonable grounds for making it. Where a party has been induced to enter a contract by an innocent misrepresentation, he may rescind the contract or claim damages[67].

---

67   *S2(2) Misrepresentation Act 1967*

MISTAKE

Generally speaking, the parties to a contract will not be relieved from the burden of their agreement simply because they have made a mistake or a bad bargain.

There are three exceptions to this rule. These are where there have been a *Common Mistake*, a *Mutual Mistake* or a *Unilateral Mistake*.

A *Common Mistake* is where both parties to an agreement *share the same fundamental error* about the circumstances surrounding the transaction. Examples include *res sua* where, unbeknownst to both parties, the subject matter of the contract is already owned by the buyer or *res extincta* where, unbeknown to both parties, the subject matter of the contract no longer exists.

Mutual Mistake occurs where the parties think they are in agreement but *believe fundamentally different versions of either the terms of the contract or the subject matter* of the contract, but they do not realise it.

Raffles v Wichelhaus (1864)

The Claimant entered into a contract to sell "125 bales of Surat cotton "to arrive ex Peerless from Bombay". It so happened that there were two ships named "*Peerless*" arriving in Liverpool from Bombay, one departing in October and another departing in December. The Defendant thought the contract was for cotton on the October ship whilst the Claimant thought the contract was for the cotton on the December ship. When the December *Peerless* arrived, the claimant tried to deliver it, however the defendant repudiated the agreement, saying that their contract was for the cotton on the October *Peerless*. The Court could not determine which ship named *Peerless* was intended in the contract, and as the two parties did not agree to the same thing, there was no binding contract.

A Unilateral Mistake occurs where *only one of the parties to the agreement is mistaken* as to a fundamental aspect of the contract, and the other party is aware of that fact.

Cundy v Lindsay (1878)

A crook named Blenkarn ordered linen handkerchiefs from Lindsay & Co. His order from a rented room at 37 Wood Street, was signed to look as if it were from Blenkiron & Co, a reputable firm known to Lindsay, who carried on business at 123 Wood Street. The goods were sent to Blenkarn, who sold them to Cundy. Lindsay successfully sued Cundy in the tort of conversion, the House of Lords ruling that Lindsay & Co had intended only to deal with Blenkiron & Co. Since there was no contract with Blenkarn because of the unilateral mistake, he received no title whatsoever to the goods, and therefore could not pass title on to Cundy.

Phillips v Brooks (1919).

A crook called Mr North selected a number of items in Phillips's jewellery shop and proposed to pay by a dud cheque for £3,000. On being informed that the goods would have to be retained until the cheque was cleared, he told the jeweller that he was Sir George Bullough of St James's Square. On checking in a directory that such a person did indeed live at that address, the jeweller permitted him to take away a valuable ring which the crook wished to take away 'for his wife's birthday tomorrow'. The crook later pawned the ring at Brooks Ltd for £350. Phillips then sued Brooks Ltd in conversion. The Court ruled that the contract between Phillips and the crook was *not void for mistake*. There had not been a mistake as to identity, but only as to the creditworthiness of the buyer. The contract had been *voidable for misrepresentation*, but the crook had passed title before Phillips took steps to avoid the contract.

The court will allow *rectification* of a contract where, perhaps through a typographical error, it does not accurately represent the intentions of the parties.

The court under the principle of *non est factum* may avoid a contract where someone, without carelessness, signs a document under a misapprehension as to its true nature or content. If the document is fundamentally different from what they thought they were signing, they may avoid its effect.

Saunders v Anglia Building Society (1970)

Mrs Gallie, a 78-year-old widow, signed a document without reading it because her spectacles were broken. She had been told by her nephew's business partner, Mr Lee, that the documents were merely to confirm a gift of her house to her nephew but in fact they were a deed of gift to Mr Lee. Mr Lee later mortgaged the property to Anglia Building Society who on Lee's default sought to repossess the house. Mrs Gallie sought to repudiate the deed of gift on the basis of *non est factum*. The House of Lords ruled in favour of Anglia on the basis that, although Mrs Gallie had not been careless, the document, being a deed of gift, was not fundamentally different from what she expected to sign.

Lloyd's Bank Plc v Waterhouse (1990)

Mr Waterhouse, who was illiterate, intended to provide a guarantee in relation to his son's purchase of a farm. In actual fact the document he signed was a guarantee in relation to all of his son's liabilities. The Court of Appeal ruled that the father could rely on *non est factum*. He had not been careless and indeed had questioned the bank manager as to the extent of his liability and the document was fundamentally different from what he expected to sign.

Chapter 15
Illegality

A contract may be vitiated on the grounds of illegality. The English courts will not enforce illegal contracts relying on the maxim, *ex turpi causa, non oritur action* (from a wrongful act, no action arises).

In *Patel v Mirza*, the Supreme Court indicated that there were two reasons for the Common Law doctrine of illegality: a person should not be allowed to profit from his own wrong-doing, and the law should be coherent, not self-defeating, and should not condone illegality. In determining whether a contract was vitiated by illegality, relevant factors for the Court included the seriousness of the conduct, its centrality to the contract, whether it was intentional, whether there was disparity in the parties' respective culpability and how serious a sanction denial of enforcement might be to the party seeking enforcement[68].

The court has the power to *sever* void clauses, excising them from the contract and permitting the remainder to be enforced.

Void clauses at Common Law include those ousting the jurisdiction of the court. Whilst by statute contracts in restraint of trade are *prima facie* void but they may be valid if it can be shown that the person who imposes the restrictions has a legitimate interest to protect, if the restriction is reasonable as

---

68   *Patel v Mirza [2016] UKSC 42*

between the parties and the restriction is not contrary to the public interest.

Patel v Mirza (2016)

Mr Patel paid £620,000 to Mr Mirza under an agreement under which Mr Mirza would bet on the price of some shares, on the basis of insider information. Using insider information to profit from trading in shares was an offence under section 52, Criminal Justice Act 1983. As it happened, the scheme did not come to fruition as expected as the insider information was mistaken. Thereafter, Mr Patel brought a claim based on contract and unjust enrichment for the return of £620,000. Mr Mirza argued that no such obligation could be enforced because the whole contract was illegal, and any claim would be precluded by the principle of ex turpi causa non oritur action. The Supreme Court ruled that Mr Patel could recover the money because it would have the effect of returning the parties to their positions prior to the conclusion of the illegal contract, as well as prevent Mr Mirza from being unjustly enriched. The Supreme Court balanced the policies that a person should not be allowed to profit from his own wrongdoing and that the law should be coherent and not self-defeating. It asked itself whether the public interest would be harmed by the enforcement of the illegal agreement, taking into account the purpose of the prohibition which has been transgressed, and whether the purpose would be enhanced by the denial of the claim, any other relevant public policy on which the denial of the claim may have an impact and whether denial of the claim would be a proportionate response to the illegality, bearing in mind that punishment is a matter for the criminal courts.

CHAPTER 16
DURESS

Duress arises where one party secures agreement by an illegitimate threat to the other party. The threat may be to the other party, his family, his employees[69] or his property[70].

Similarly, the law recognises economic duress to a person's financial wellbeing.

---

69   *Royal Boskalis v Mountain [1999]*
70   *Skeate v Beale (1840)*

Universe Tankships Inc of Monrovia v International Transport Workers [1983]

The International Transport Workers' Federation black-listed a Universe Tankship ship. To secure the release of the ship, Universe Tankships Inc agreed to pay $6,480 into ITWF's welfare fund. The House of Lords ruled that economic duress could be seen from lack of any practicable choice but to submit.

Pao On v Lau Yiu [1979]

Long Lau Yiu Long and his younger brother Benjamin were engaging in a share swap deal with Pao On and his family. Pao demanded that instead of that, Lau would indemnify him if the share price fell below $2.50, threatening that unless he got this "guarantee agreement", he would not complete the main contract. Wishing to avoid bad publicity, Lau signed. When Pao tried to enforce the guarantee agreement. Lau argued that the guarantee was procured by duress. The Privy Council ruled that this was no more than ordinary commercial pressure. Factors which were relevant to distinguish between ordinary commercial pressure and economic duress were whether the victim protested at the time, whether they take steps to avoid the contract after it was formed, whether they had access to independent legal advice and whether they had a realistic alternative course of action at the time.

The threat must be illegitimate. Illegitimate threats include threats to commit a crime, a tort, a breach of contract. A statement of facts or a threat to sue may seem threatening but are not illegitimate (although a threat to prosecute may be).

Duress renders a contract voidable at the instance of the innocent party. It is not possible to contractually exclude a challenge on the basis of duress[71].

---

71   *Borelli v Ting [2010]*

Chapter 17
Undue Influence

Undue influence arises where on party abuses a relation-ship of influence over the other or a vulnerability of the other to achieve an improper advantage[72].

Williams v Bayley (1866)

Mr Bayley's son forged his father's signature on promissory notes and gave them to Mr Williams. Mr Williams threatened Mr Bayley that he would bring criminal prosecution against his son unless he granted an equitable mortgage securing the notes. The House of Lords ruled that the mortgage be cancelled on the grounds of undue influence on the grounds that the father was influenced by the threat.

Under influence may be presumed if a *"special relationship"* of trust between the parties such as between a parent and child while still a minor, a guardian and ward, a religious adviser and follower, a doctor and patient and between a solicitor and his client. No such presumption arises between spouses[73].

---

72   *CIBC Mortgages v Pitt (1994)*
73   *Royal Bank of Scotland v Etridge (No 2) [2001]*

Even where no presumption arises, a party may rely on undue influence if they can prove that they are in a relationship of trust and confidence in which they are subservient to the other. The transaction itself may call for explanation if it is not reasonably to be accounted for on the grounds of charity, friendship, relationship or other ordinary motives on which ordinary men act[74].

Contracts with third parties may be affected by the undue influence if they have constructive knowledge of it. This may

---

74   *Royal Bank of Scotland v Etridge (No 2) [2001]*

arise where the transaction on its face is not to the financial advantages of one of the parties and there is a substantial risk of it being obtained by undue influence.

Royal Bank of Scotland v Etridge (No 2) (2001)

Mrs Etridge had mortgaged her property to a bank to secure a loan that was used by her husband for his business. Her husband's business had failed, and the wife had alleged that she had been under undue influence to sign the security agreement. The House of Lords ruled that a bank (or its solicitor) is "put on inquiry" (fixed with constructive knowledge) that there may be the risk of undue influence or misrepresentation, if they transact for security over a domestic home, and the loan will only benefit one person and not the other. The bank could have avoided this if it ensured that the non-benefiting party received independent advice from a solicitor.

CHAPTER 18
DISCHARGE

A contract is discharged in one of four ways: it may be discharged by agreement, by performance, by frustration or by breach.

As a general rule, discharge by performance requires complete and exact performance of all the obligations in the contract.

> **Re Moore & Co and Landauer & Co's arbitration (1921)**
> A contract for the sale of 3,100 tins of peaches described the tins as being packed in cases of 30. When they arrived some of the tins were packed in cases of 24 although the agreed overall number of tins was supplied. The Court of Appeal ruled that the purchaser was entitled to reject the goods as they were not as described.

There are a number of exceptions which lessen the potential harshness of this rule.

Where a buyer deals as a consumer and the breach is so slight that it is unreasonable to reject the goods, the breach is treated as a breach of warranty and will not now entitle the buyer to reject the goods[75]. Further, the full performance is not required to discharge the contract: 1) where the obligations are severable (for example if payment is due from time

---

75   *Ss 15A and 30(2A), Sale of Goods Act 1979*

to time as part of the contract is performed[76]); 2) where the contract is capable of being fulfilled by substantial performance (in which case the cost of the incomplete work can be deducted[77]); 3) where performance has been prevented by the other party[78]; 4) where partial performance has been accepted by the other party; or 5) if the co-operation of the other party is needed to perform the contract its tender of performance, that is to say its offer to perform the contractual obligations, is rejected.

Parties may agree to discharge their contract. Where the contractual obligations are yet to be performed, the mutual exchange of promises to release one another from future performance will be sufficient consideration. Where the contract is partly or fully performed the other party must provide consideration in order to be released from performing their part of the contract: this is known as *accord and satisfaction*.

A breach of contract may occur in three ways: 1) where a party fails to perform their contractual obligation; 2) where a party performs their obligation in a defective manner; and, 3) where a party, prior to the time of performance, states that they will not fulfil their contractual obligations.

---

76   *Roberts v Havelock (1832)*
77   *H Dakin & Co v Lee (1916), Bolton v Mahdeva (1972)*
78   *Planche v Coburn (1831)*

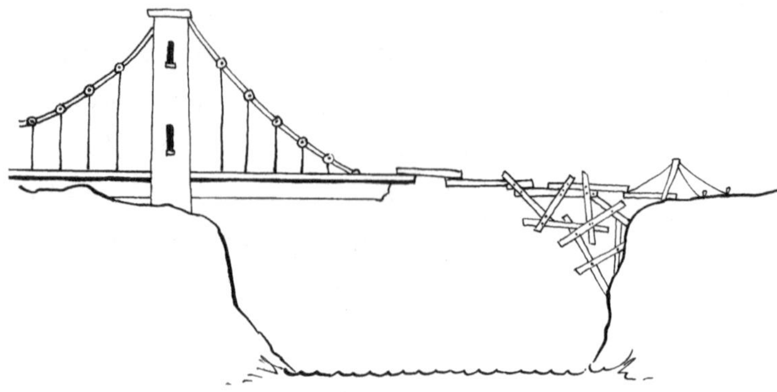

Any breach will result in the innocent party being able to sue for damages. However, where there has been a repudiatory breach (a serious breach of a condition) and the breach gives the right to treat the agreement as discharged, the innocent party can elect either to refuse either to perform their part of the contract, or to continue the contract. The breach may be actual or anticipatory. Anticipatory breach arises where one party, prior to the actual due date of performance, demonstrates an intention not to perform their contractual obligations. Anticipatory breaches may be express or implied. The innocent party can sue for damages immediately or wait until the actual time for performance before taking action.

Late performance will not amount to a sufficient breach to repudiate the contract, unless time is stipulated to be or becomes "of the essence".

Finally, a contract will be discharged by reason of frustration where performance of the contract becomes impossible.

Examples of frustrating events include: 1) where the subject matter of the contract has been destroyed; 2) where government interference, or supervening illegality, prevents performance; 3) where a particular event, which is the sole reason for the contract, fails to take place; 4) the commercial purpose of the contract is defeated; and 5) in the case of a contract of personal service where the party dies or becomes otherwise incapacitated.

There will be no frustration however where the parties have made an express provision in the contract for the event which has occurred (for example by a force majeure clause), or the frustrating event is self-induced, or an alternative method of performance is still possible or the contract has simply become more expensive to perform.

Krell v Henry [1903]

Mr Paul Krell agreed to rent to CS Henry a third floor flat at 56A Pall Mall so he could watch the coronation procession of Edward VII scheduled for 26 and 27 June 1902. Henry agreed £75 for the two days and paid a deposit of £25. The procession did not take place on the days originally set, on the grounds that the King was suffering from appendicitis. Henry refused to pay the remaining £50. Krell sued and Henry counterclaimed for the return of his deposit. The Court of Appeal held that the contract was frustrated and Henry was not liable to pay for the room.

At Common Law, the effect of frustration is to make the contract void as from the time of the frustrating event.

The Law Reform (Frustrated Contracts) Act 1943 sought to address the potential hardship caused by this. The Act provides that upon frustration, money paid is recoverable and money due to be paid ceases to be payable. The parties may be permitted, at the discretion of the court, to retain expenses incurred from any money received, or recover those expenses from money due to be paid before the frustrating event. Where a party has gained a valuable benefit under the contract he may, at the discretion of the court, be required to pay a reasonable sum in respect of it.

Chapter 19
Remedies

Damages for breach of contract are designed to put the parties in the position they would have been in had the contract been performed.

To be recoverable, the loss must have been caused by the breach of contract and not be too remote from this; damages will only be awarded in respect of losses which arise naturally from the breach or which both parties may reasonably be supposed to have contemplated, when the contract was made, as a probable result of its breach[79].Whilst the nature of the loss needs to be foreseeable, the scale of the loss does not have to be[80].

Hadley v Baxendale (1854)

Mr Hadley was a miller and meal man in partnership as City Steam-Mills in Gloucester. The crankshaft of the steam engine at their mill had broken and Mr Hadley arranged to have a new one made by W. Joyce & Co. in Greenwich. To ensure they had a template for the new crankshaft, W. Joyce & Co. needed to see the broken crankshaft and Mr Hadley hired Pickford & Co, a firm of common carriers run by Mr Baxendale to deliver the crankshaft to W. Joyce & Co. Due to Mr Baxendale's late delivery of the crankshaft,

---

79   *Hadley v Baxendale (1854), The Heron II (1969)*
80   *The Achilleas, Transfield Shipping v Mercator Shipping [2008]*

Mr Hadley sued for the profits he lost due to the late delivery. The Court refused Mr Hadley's claim for lost profits, holding that Mr Baxendale could only be held liable for losses that were generally foreseeable "in the ordinary course of things", or if Mr Hadley had warned Mr Baxendale in advance that he would lose business if the delivery was not made promptly. The mere fact that a party is sending something to be repaired does not indicate that the party would lose profits if it is not delivered on time.

The innocent party has a duty to take reasonable steps to mitigate any loss he suffers as a result of the breach; where losses could have been reasonably avoided, they will not be recoverable[81].

In awarding damages, the court seeks to put a party in the position he would have been in had the contract been performed. This may be the value of the goods bought or the market value if this is higher than that stipulated in the contract. Where defective goods or services are provided, the award of damages may represent the cost of cure or the difference between the value of the goods or services received and those paid for.

---

81   *Pilkington v Wood (1953)*

Ruxley Electronics v Forsyth (1996)

Ruxley agreed to build a swimming pool in Forsyth's garden. The contract specified that the pool would have a diving area seven feet, six inches deep. When constructed, the diving area was only six feet deep. This was still a safe depth for diving and one which did not affect the value of the pool. Forsyth was not happy, however, and he brought an action for breach of contract claiming the cost of having a pool demolished and rebuilt (the cost of cure), at a sum of £21,540. The House of Lords ruled that Forsyth was only entitled to £2500 for loss of amenity, saying that the law must cater for those occasions where the value of the promise to the promisee exceeds the financial enhancement of his position which full performance will secure. The court must look to the loss truly suffered.

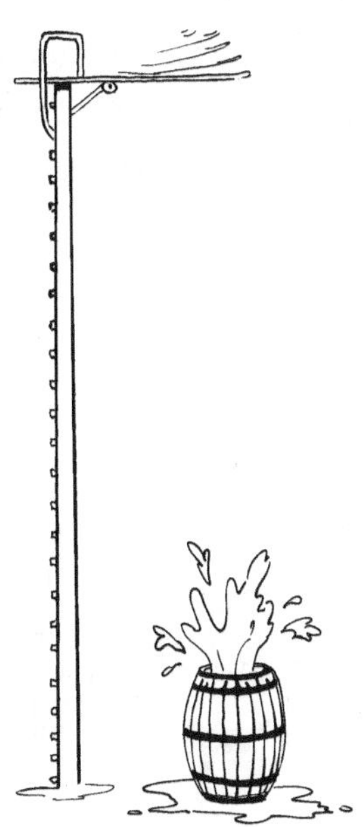

Where it is impossible to determine the sum needed to put the claimant in the position he would have been in, had the contract been performed, the Court will instead award a sum reflecting the loss caused by his reliance on the contract and will seek to put the claimant in the position he would have been in had the contract never been made.

Anglia Television v Reed (1972)

Anglia asked Robert Reed (the actor who portrayed the father, Mike Brady, in "The Brady Bunch") to star in their TV film, *The Man in the Wood*, about an American man married to an English woman who has an adventure in an English wood. Unfortunately, Mr Reed withdrew just before filming was about to start as he was booked to do a play in the USA. Anglia cancelled the film. Anglia did not claim for loss of profits, because that was too uncertain but instead they claimed their wasted expenditure. The Court of Appeal ruled that expenditure incurred could be claimed, so long as it was within the contemplation of the parties.

Where there has been a breach of trust, the Court has required that profits to be handed over:

Attorney General v Blake (2000)

Mr George Blake had been a member of the Secret Service (MI6) and given the nature of his work had signed the Official Secrets Act 1911 to always keep his activities secret. He was later to become a Soviet double agent and on his discovery was sent to Wormwood Scubs prison. He escaped and fled to the Soviet Union. He wrote an autobiography called *"No Other Choice"*. Whilst the material in the book was no longer secret, the UK Government sued him for the money he was to receive from his publishers, Jonathan Cape Ltd. The House of Lords ruled that in exceptional cases, when the normal remedy is inadequate to compensate for breach of contract, the court can order the defendant to account for all profits. This was just such an exceptional case.

Exceptionally, the Court may also award damages for injury to feelings, mental distress and loss of amenity where the purpose of the contract, rather than being purely commercial, was to provide pleasure.

Jarvis v Swan Tours (1973)

Mr. Jarvis was a solicitor working at Barking Council. Reading a holiday brochure from Swan Tours, he booked a holiday in Morialp, Switzerland. The brochure promised "a wonderland of sun, snow and ice", with a wide variety of fine ski-runs, a skating rink and an "exhilarating toboggan run". It promised a friendly welcome at the hotel from Herr Weibel "the charming owner who speaks English" and that its own Alphütte Bar was "open several evenings a week". It promised "a great time, when you book this house party holiday" and that there would be "a welcome party on arrival, afternoon tea and cake for 7 days and yodeller evening". An added option included the hire of ski equipment and tuition. Mr Jarvis booked 15 days and took the ski package. The reality was rather different. He found the "house party" was only 13 people in the first week and none in the second week. Mr Weibel could not speak English. So, there was Mr Jarvis, in the second week, in this hotel with no house party at all, and no one could speak English, except himself. He was very disappointed, also with the ski-ing. It was some distance away and there were only mini-skis and the boots chaffed his feet. There were no Swiss cakes, just crisps and little dry nut cakes. The "yodeller" was a local man who came in work clothes and sang four or five songs quickly. The "Alphütte Bar" was only open for one evening and even then it was empty. Mr Jarvis sued for breach of contract. The Court of Appeal ruled that Mr Jarvis could recover damages for the cost of his holiday, but also damages for "disappointment, the distress, the upset and frustration caused by the breach."

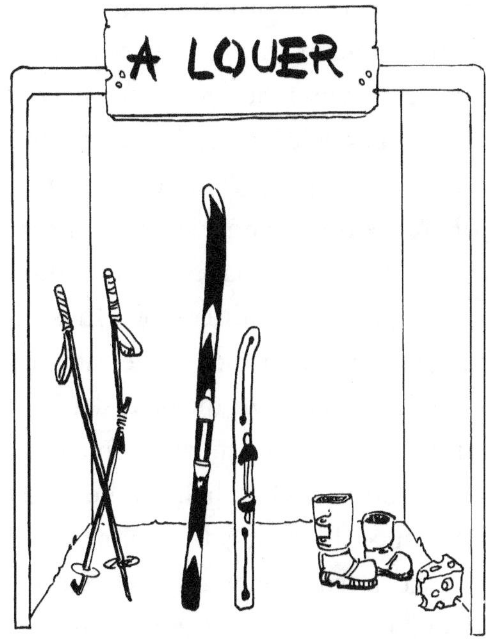

The parties to an agreement may make provisions for the amount of damages that will have to be paid in the event of any breach occurring. The Court will however not enforce terms which amount to a penalty; a clause will be a penalty if it imposes a detriment on the contract-breaker out of all proportion to any legitimate interest of the innocent party in the enforcement of the primary obligation rather than simply punishing the defaulter[82].

Through an order for specific performance, a party in breach may be instructed to complete their part of the contract. Unlike an award for damages, an order for specific performance does not automatically flow from a breach of contract.

---

82   *Cavendish Square Holding BV v Makdessi [2015]*

An order of specific performance will only be granted in cases where the Common Law remedy of damages is inadequate. This may be because the goods being sold are unique[83] or have been specifically identified[84] or where the remedy in damages would be inadequate[85]. Specific performance will not be granted where the court cannot supervise its enforcement.

Moreover, specific performance is an equitable remedy which the court grants at its discretion. Thus, the claimant must be willing to perform his side of the bargain and performance must still be possible for the defendant and not cause undue hardship[86]. As it is an equitable remedy, the claimant "must come to equity with clean hands"; the Court can refuse specific performance if it thinks the claimant has acted improperly[87] or has delayed unduly seeking a remedy[88].

Another equitable remedy of the court is to grant an injunction ordering a person not to break their contract. Breach is punishable as a contempt of court by fine or imprisonment.

---

83   *Philips v Lamdin (1949)*
84   *Section 52(1) Sale of Goods Act 1979*
85   *Beswick v Beswick (1968)*
86   *Patel v Ali (1984)*
87   *Walters v Morgan (1861)*
88   *Milward v Earl of Thanet (1801)*

CHAPTER 20
EPILOGUE

Unlike some countries where the law is simply stated in a code, English law is found in statute, precedent case law and even custom.

English law has been allowed to benefit from insights over many centuries but has also evolved to fit the needs of a changing world. This has enabled English law to develop its own rich patina painted by real human experience.

Thus, we have reasonableness judged by the standards of the *reasonable man on the Clapham Omnibus.*

And thus, in *Donoghue v Stevenson*, one Mrs Donoghue sued for nervous shock she suffered on the discovery of a snail in her ginger beer bottle when out on a date in a Paisley café and thereby created the *tort of negligence*.

Yet for all its curiosities, English law remains the preferred choice of law for most international contracts and the bulk of the business of the English High Court is occupied with cases from around the world.

Glossary
Some common contract terms and what they do

What the terms says	What it does
Subject to contract	**This is a non-binding draft and not the final contract between the parties.**
WHEREAS the Seller and the Buyer are desirous of agreeing terms for the conduct of their business	**"a recital": This does not form part of the contract but provides background to help the reader interpret the contract.**
No variation of this agreement shall be effective unless it is in writing and signed by the parties (or their authorised representatives).	**The agreement may only be amended by the parties recording the change in writing; this ensures that variations are properly recorded.**
If any term of this Agreement is, in whole or in part, held to be illegal or unenforceable to any extent under any enactment or rule of law, that term or part shall to that extent be deemed not to form part of this Agreement and the enforceability of the remainder of this Agreement shall not be affected.	**A "blue pencil clause": The contract is not defeated by the illegality of a clause, instead the clause is treated as if omitted.**

This agreement is governed by and shall be construed in accordance with the laws of England.	**A choice of law clause: Note that the choice of law to apply to the agreement here is the law of England rather than the law, say, of the United Kingdom. This is important as the law of England is different from the laws of Scotland and Wales.**
In this agreement, unless the context clearly indicates another intention: *(a) reference to one gender includes all other genders,* *(b) reference to the singular includes the plural and vice versa,* *(c) reference to a clause, schedule or party is a reference to a clause of or a schedule or party to this agreement,* *(d) reference to a statutory provision is a reference to that provision as modified or re-enacted or both from time to time and to any subordinate legislation made under the statutory provision,* *(e) reference to writing includes fax, e-mail and similar means of communication,* *(f) any reference to a person includes natural persons and partnerships, firms and other such unincorporated bodies, corporate bodies and all other legal persons of whatever kind and however constituted.*	**An interpretation clause: This clause sets out some basic rules to help the reader when trying to understand the contract.**

The parties to this agreement submit to the exclusive jurisdiction of the English Courts.	**A choice of forum clause: The parties have agreed to have any dispute decided before the English courts.**
In consideration of the Lender making the Loan to the Borrower under this agreement, and for other good and valuable consideration, the receipt and adequacy of which is acknowledged, the Guarantor unconditionally guarantees to the Lender the payment when due of all sums payable now or in the future to the Lender by the Borrower under this loan or in connection with it, and undertakes with the Lender that, if and whenever the Borrower is in default in the payment of any sum whatsoever under this agreement or in connection with it, the Guarantor will on demand pay such sum.	**A guarantee: The Guarantor agrees to pay the Borrower's debt if he defaults.**
In consideration of the Lender making the Loan to the Borrower under this agreement, and for other good and valuable consideration, the receipt and adequacy of which is acknowledged, the Guarantor guarantees to the Lender that the Guarantor will, on demand discharge the Loan as primary obligor and not only as guarantor.	**An indemnity: Here the Guarantor additionally agrees to be co-debtor with the Borrower for the Borrower's debt. The Lender can simply demand the money back direct from the Guarantor and not wait to see if the Borrower defaults.**

Save as expressly provided for in this agreement, this agreement does not and is not intended to afford any third party the right to enforce its terms whether under the Contracts (Rights of Third Parties) Act 1999 or otherwise.	**Only parties to the contract can enjoy the benefit of it.**
No Party shall issue or make any public announcement or disclose any information regarding this agreement unless prior to such public announcement or disclosure unless it furnishes all the Parties with a copy of such announcement or disclosure and obtains the approval of all the Parties as to its terms. However, no Party shall be prohibited from issuing or making any such public announcement or disclosing such information if it is necessary to do so to comply with any applicable law or the regulations of a recognised stock exchange.	**This clause ensures that one party does not press release news about the agreement without first reaching agreement with the other side as to what it says.**
This agreement embodies the entire understanding and agreement between the parties and neither party is relying on any representations, promises, terms, conditions or obligations oral or written express or implied other than those contained in this agreement.	**An entire agreement clause. This records that all the terms and representations between the parties are recorded in the agreement.**

This agreement may be executed in any number of counterparts, each of which when executed and delivered shall constitute a duplicate original, but all the counterparts shall together constitute the one agreement.	**The parties don't have to all sign the same document; they can sign copies. This allows parties to execute the agreement remotely.**
Any notice required to be given for the purposes of this agreement must be given by sending it by pre-paid first class post or fax, or by delivery by hand at the relevant address shown in this agreement or such other address as has been notified in accordance with this clause by the party concerned as being their address for the purposes of this clause. Any notice sent by post shall be deemed to have been served 2 days after posting. In proving service, it shall be sufficient to prove that a notice was properly addressed and stamped and put into the post. Any notice sent by fax shall be deemed to have been served on the next business day following the date of despatch of it. Any notice delivered by hand shall be deemed to have been served when physically delivered at the relevant address.	**A notice clause: If one party follows the procedure set out, the other side cannot later pretend it has not been given proper notice.**

The Contractor warrants, represents and undertakes that it has obtained all necessary and required licences, consents and permits to perform the Services.	**This is a warranty. Here the contractor is warranting to the other party that he can undertake the services legally.**
The Seller undertakes to indemnify and keep indemnified the Buyer against any and all losses and liabilities up to the amount of £1,000,000 (one million pounds) calculated on a pound for pound basis (including damages, claims, demands, proceedings and penalties) which may be suffered or incurred by it by reason of any defect in or challenge to the Seller's title in the Product	**An indemnity clause; here the Seller agrees to compensate the Buyer for any losses the Buyer may suffer from a challenge to the Seller's ownership of the goods being sold.**
Neither Party shall have any liability under or be deemed to be in breach of this Agreement for any delays or failures in performance of this Agreement that result from circumstances beyond the reasonable control of that Party. The Party affected by such circumstances shall promptly notify the other Party in writing when such circumstances cause a delay or failure in performance and when they cease to do so. If such circumstances exist for a continuous period of more than 6 months, either Party may terminate this Agreement by written notice to the other Party.	**A force majeure clause: rather the contract being frustrated, the parties may delay performance if they are prevented by external factors.**

Neither Party shall be liable to the other Party in contract, tort, negligence, breach of statutory duty or otherwise for any loss, damage, costs or expenses of any nature whatsoever incurred or suffered by that other Party of an indirect or consequential nature including without limitation any economic loss or other loss of turnover, profits, business or goodwill. Nothing in this Agreement excludes liability for fraud or in negligence for damages for causing personal injury or death.	**An exclusion clause: The parties exclude their liability to each other under the contract and in tort (except for fraud and negligently caused death or personal injuries which can't be excluded.)**
Completion shall take place on the Completion Date at the offices of the Buyers' Solicitors or such other place as may be agreed in writing by the Buyers and the Seller. At Completion:....	**A completion clause: The parties have chosen a specific time and date for key steps to be performed under the agreement. The actions to take place on completion are then listed.**
Any dispute, agreement controversy, or claim arising out of or in connection with this agreement, or the breach, termination or validity thereof, shall be submitted to the [Chartered Institute of Arbitrators (CIArb)] and settled by final and binding arbitration in accordance with the [CIArb Arbitration Rules]. Judgment on any award issued under this provision may be entered by any court of competent jurisdiction.	**An arbitration clause: The parties elect to have their dispute resolved by arbitration.**

This agreement shall not constitute or imply any partnership, joint venture, agency, fiduciary relationship or other relationship between the Parties other than the contractual relationship expressly provided for in this agreement. Neither Party shall have, nor represent that it has, any authority to make any commitments on the other Party's behalf.	**This clause is designed to prevent the agreement being interpreted as creating a relationship of agency or partnership between the parties. By including this in the agreement neither party can commit or speak for the other party.**
Each Party ('Receiving Party') shall keep the Confidential Information of the other Party ('Supplying Party') confidential and secret, whether disclosed to or received by the Receiving Party. The Receiving Party shall only use the Confidential Information of the Supplying Party for the Purpose and for performing the Receiving Party's obligations under the agreement. The obligations of confidentiality shall not apply to any information which: (a) was known or in the possession of the Receiving Party before it was provided to the Receiving Party by the Providing Party; (b) is, or becomes, publicly available through no fault of the Receiving Party; (c) is required to be disclosed by order of a court of competent jurisdiction.	**A confidentiality clause.**

Each party shall (at its own expense) promptly execute and deliver all such documents, and do all such things, or procure the execution of documents and doing of such things as are required to give full effect to this agreement and the transaction intended to be effected pursuant to it.	**The parties will take any steps necessary to ensure that the agreement is performed (even where that step has not been expressly spelled out in the terms).**
Except as expressively provided in this agreement, each party shall pay its own costs and expenses incurred in connection with the preparation, negotiation and execution of this agreement and the documents referred to in it.	**Each party agrees to pay their own costs of drafting the agreement.**
Time shall be of the essence for the purposes of any provision of this agreement.	**A time of the essence clause: Unless it is agreed that time will be of the essence, a party can only recover damages if the agreement is performed late and cannot repudiate the agreement.**
Neither Party may assign, delegate, sub-contract, mortgage, charge or otherwise transfer any or all of its rights and obligations under this agreement without the prior written agreement of the other Party.	**Neither party may assign their rights under the agreement to someone else.**

Without prejudice to other remedies or rights, either Party may terminate this agreement at any time by written notice to the other Party ('Other Party') and the notice taking effect as specified in the notice: *(a) if the Other Party is in material breach of its obligations under this agreement, and where a breach is capable of remedy within 14 days, the breach is not remedied with 14 days by the Other Party receiving notice which specifies the breach and requiring the breach to be remedied; or* *(b) if the Other Party becomes insolvent or if an order is made or a resolution is passed for the winding up of the Other Party (other than voluntarily for the purpose of solvent amalgamation or re-construction), or if an administrator, administrative receiver or receiver is appointed in respect of the whole or any part of the Other Party's assets or business, or if the Other Party makes any composition with its creditors or takes or suffers any similar or analogous action in consequence of debt.*	**A termination clause.**

NOTES

www.ingramcontent.com/pod-product-compliance
Lightning Source LLC
Chambersburg PA
CBHW061006050726
47592CB00003B/1362